# The Capture and Execution of John Brown

# Also from Westphalia Press
# westphaliapress.org

# The Capture and
# Execution
# of John Brown
# A Tale of Martyrdom

## by Elijah Avey

WESTPHALIA PRESS
An Imprint of Policy Studies Organization

Westphalia Press
An imprint of Policy Studies Organization
1527 New Hampshire Ave., NW
Washington, D.C. 20036
info@ipsonet.org

ISBN-13: 978-1-63391-591-6
ISBN-10: 1-63391-591-3

Cover design by Jeffrey Barnes:
jbarnesbook.design

Daniel Gutierrez-Sandoval, Executive Director
PSO and Westphalia Press

Updated material and comments on this edition
can be found at the Westphalia Press website:
www.westphaliapress.org

JOHN BROWN.

# THE
# Capture and Execution

OF

# John Brown

*A TALE OF MARTYRDOM*

BY

## ELIJAH AVEY

EYE WITNESS

———

*With Thirty Illustrations*

———

PRINTED BY THE
BRETHREN PUBLISHING HOUSE, ELGIN, ILL.
FOR THE AUTHOR AND PUBLISHER
ELIJAH AVEY
*Address:* STATION M, CHICAGO, ILL.

To my Grandson

John G. Wilson

I affectionately dedicate this book

# CONTENTS.

# LIST OF ILLUSTRATIONS.

# THE CAPTURE AND
# EXECUTION OF
# JOHN BROWN.

# CHAPTER I.

Six o'clock, Monday morning, October 17, 1859, was one of the most thrilling moments of my life.

I was a boy at the time, learning the watch-maker's trade at Charlestown, Jefferson County, Virginia. At that hour, on that historic day, I was awakened by the long roll of drums and the strident notes of fifes calling "Assembly!" Hastily dressing myself, I rushed to the street and the first person I encountered was John Moore, sheriff of the county, who was hurriedly saddling his horse and whose countenance betrayed great agitation. Looking down the street in the direction of the court house, I discerned two companies of the home militia, the Botts Grays, and what was popularly known as "Captain Rowens Company," all in uniform and assembling amid scenes of the greatest confusion and excitement. Turning to Sheriff Moore as he was preparing to mount his horse I asked him the reason for all this tumult and display of force. His reply was:

"Harper's Ferry is in possession of a band of unknown men." With all of a boy's curiosity and with the contagious excitement warming the blood in my veins, I hurried to the court house and mingled with the gathering crowd. The news of the attack on Harper's Ferry had spread like wildfire. Vague rumors of a "Yankee" invasion filled the air and emotional men and women were beside themselves with frantic excitement. People living in the country fled from their homes and gathered in town for the feeling of security that numbers gave. Among them were the wealthy and aristocratic slave owners of the section and for that day, at least, the negroes on the plantations were masters of all they surveyed.

Never before in a time of peace, had our quiet little town been the scene of such intense popular feeling. In less time than it takes to tell it almost every man and boy in Charestown, who was able to carry a gun, was equipped with some kind of a weapon and ready to go to Harper's Ferry for the purpose of capturing or killing the bold intruders who had so ruthlessly disturbed the peace of the country side.

At 9 o'clock the troops and armed citizens marched to the Winchester and Harper's Ferry railroad depot and there waited for the regular train to come in from Winchester. When it arrived they took charge of the train, ordered the astonished passengers, who knew nothing of the trouble, to disembark. Many of the travellers were very much frightened and all of them repaired to the hotels and private homes, to obtain shelter until the "cruel war was over." In the evening the train returned and the passengers, relieved somewhat of their fears, continued their interrupted journeys to their various destinations.

On the departure of the militia a thousand vague, nameless fears, seemed to take possession of the populace. Many of them could not see the political aspect of an attack on Harper's Ferry; few of them realized that a stupendous tragedy was soon to be enacted at their thresholds, none of them dreamed that the fields of Antietam, the slopes of South Mountain or the embattled crags of Maryland Heights were soon to be strewn with mangled corpses—that the limpid waters of

the beautiful Shenandoah would be dyed
with human blood, that the peaceful homes
along the valley of the Potomac would soon
be consumed by the fire brands of civil
war. All that the people thought was that
a band of desperadoes, an organized body
of robbers had spread the rumor of an attack on Harper's Ferry, or had attacked
that point as a cunning ruse to draw the
able bodied men of rich old Charlestown
away from its corporate limits, leaving it
unprotected and defenseless and while in
this state they could rush in, rob the banks,
loot the stores and ransack the homes of
the wealthy for plunder—getting away to
some safe rendezvous before the men of
the town could get back. This fear grew
to a certainty and at 1 o'clock Lawyer
Hunter called a meeting of the men and
boys who had not gone to Harper's Ferry.
They assembled at the court house and it
was resolved that all should get guns and
guard the town. This was done. The stay-
at-homes were organized as patrols; and a
man named Warrick and myself were de-
tailed to guard the two blocks approaching
the railroad station. The strain on the
home guard, as the night wore on, was in-

tense, but at midnight a dispatch was received from Harper's Ferry which threw the first ray of true light on the situation. The message stated that a band of abolitionists, led by John Brown, the famous "Ossawattomie Brown," of Kansas, as they called him had made a raid on Harper's Ferry. The news relieved the suspense. The veil had been lifted, the intense feeling of fear of an unknown and dreaded enemy was dissipated and at the hour when ghosts are supposed to walk, my companion and I got our honorable discharges as high privates in the war of Harper's Ferry, and relieved of the fearful responsibilities of sentry duty, we went to our homes and succeeded in snatching about five hours sleep before the dawn of another exciting day.

It is at this point, Ladies and Gentlemen, that I am about to unveil one of the greatest historic paintings of the age,—a picture of dramatic interest—revealing a scene sombre in its tragedy and one, which, in the light of today—is pregnant in its meaning. It is the picture of a scene in the last act in the life of that man of iron, that strange old hero, whose turbulent and stormy history is so woven in the annals of the border wars of Missouri and Kansas, that his name is written on every one of its bloody pages. It is a picture of a lion wounded to death, of an unconquered soul in chains, of a hero sapped of strength, but the incarnation of courage. "The Imprisonment of John Brown." No longer the foe of the border ruffians—now the hero of the militant abolitionists—soon to be the martyr of a principle for which he dared to do and die.

He was the victim of his own fanaticism. With a handful of men, 22 in all he tried to free a race of slaves and the climax of his daring was his capture, at Harper's Ferry, at 7 o'clock, Tuesday morning, Oct. 18, 1859, by a company of ninety marine soldiers from Washington, D. C., with two pieces of artillery and led by Con'l Robert E. Lee a 1 Lieutenant J. E. B. Stuart. With hi 1 were taken Aaron D. Stevens, his comrade, and three other followers.

These men were placed in the old jail at Charlestown about 5 o'clock in the afternoon of the day of their capture.

"THE IMPRISONMENT OF JOHN BROWN"

Copyrighted 1904 and 1906 by Elijah Avey, originator and proprietor

The picture which is now before you shows John Brown, in his prison cell at Charlestown, Jefferson County, Virginia, eight miles from Harper's Ferry. It is historically correct, being painted from an actual sketch taken at the time, October 25th, and which is a part of my Museum of relics of John Brown. In the foreground of the picture, lying wounded on the floor is "John" Brown, the companion of Jim Lane and the hero of many a free-state battle. Beside him lies his old bible. The wound across his nose was inflicted by the sword of Lieutenant Stuart during the fight in the engine house. Brown also was stabbed in his left arm and once in the body with the soldiers bayonets.

Stevens, the brave comrade of Brown's a remarkably handsome man, lies in the middle ground. The wound on his forehead was a glance shot from one of the marines. It was quite severe and for a long time he lay at the point of death. He also had a bayonet wound in the breast. No. 1 to the left. The soldier with the gun is the jail guard. No. 2 is Lieutenant Stuart of Washington, D. C., who helped to capture Brown and his men. No. 3 is

Senator Mason of Virginia, a person of historic interest. He was one of the principal figures in the Mason and Slydell incident, whose capture aboard an English vessel on the high seas in the spring of 1862, almost led to war with England. He was held for a time by the federal government but was finally released. No. 4 is Governor Wise of Virginia. He was a red-hot secessionist and declared, previous to the election of Lincoln, that in the event Lincoln was successful in his race for the presidency that "he would not remain in the union one hour," and who declared that if John C. Fremont was elected he would march the militia of Virginia upon Washington and sieze the capitol and national archives.

No. 5 is the reported. No. 6 is Sheriff John Moore reading the warrant to Brown on the morning of Oct. 25th, to appear in court for his trial. No. 7 is White of New York, one of Cooks attorneys. No. 8, the man with his arm resting on the table, is the deputy jailor, James Campbell.

Boy as I was, the fateful events of those days impressed me greatly. I attended the trial of John Brown and those of his comrades. Many persons called to see Brown

John Brown's birth-place at Torrington, Connecticut, where he lived until five years old, when his father moved to Hudson, Ohio. It is now owned by the John Brown Historical Society at Torrington.

during his captivity and, in discussing his act, he would tell them that what he had done toward liberating the negroes from slavery was only the beginning of what was coming. On the morning of Oct. 25, 1859, I saw him taken from the jail to the court house. Six men conveyed him on a stretcher to the trial room and the route from the jail to the court house was lined with armed soldiers who were massed shoulder to shoulder. The stretcher on which he reclined was placed close to the railing, near the attorney's desks. I remember at the time that there was some contention at the opening of the trial, between Brown's counsel, and Andrew Hunter the state's attorney. Loud language was used and the scene was so violent that it agitated Brown, who placed his left hand on the railing, and weakly drew his emaciated form up so that he could face the state's attorney, and with flashing eye and cold, even tones, exclaimed, "Gentlemen, it is no use whatever to hold the mockery of a trial over me!" Take me out and hang me at once!" While he was speaking the court room was so silent that one could hear a pin drop. When he had finished he dropped back on his couch exhausted, **his** trial proceeding.

When his papers were brought into court to be identified, he said: "I will identify any of my handwriting, and save all trouble. ı am ready to face the music." When a defense of insanity was suggested rather than interposed, he repelled it with indignation. When after his conviction, he was suddenly brought into court on the 2nd of November to listen to the judgment and directed to stand up and say why sentence should not be passed upon him.

### HIS ADDRESS TO THE COURT.

Though taken by surprise and somewhat confused, he spoke gently and tenderly as follows: and his low well modulated voice reached every corner of the court room in the death-like silence. He began, I have may it please the court, a few words to say.

"In the first place, I deny everything but what I have all along admitted, the design on my part to free the slaves. I intended certainly to have made a clear thing of that matter as I did last winter, when I went into Missouri and there took slaves without the snapping of a gun on either side. Moved them through the country and finally left them in Canada. I desired to have done the same thing again on a larger scale. That was all I intended, I never did intend murder, or treason, or the destruction of property or to excite or incite slaves to rebellion or to make insurrectin.

"I have another objection and that is, it is unjust that I should suffer such a penalty. Had I interfered in the manner which I admit has been fairly proved, for I admire the truthfulness and candor of the greater portion of the witnesses who have testified in this case, had I so interfered in behalf of the rich, the powerful, the intelligent, the so-called great, or in behalf of any of their friends, either father, mother, brother, sister, wife or children, or any of that class and suffered and sacrificed what I have in this interference, it would have been all right and every man in this court would have deemed it an act worthy of reward, rather than punishment.

"This court acknowledges as I suppose, the validity of the law of God. I see a book kissed here which I suppose to be the Bible, or at least the new testament, that teaches me that all things whatsoever I would that men should do unto me, I

should do even so to them; it teaches me
further, to remember those that are in
bonds as bound with them; I endeavored
to act upon that instruction, I say I am yet
too young to understand that God is any
respector of persons. I believe that to have
interfered as I have done, as I have freely
admitted I have done in behalf of the
despised poor, was not wrong but right.

Now if it is deemed necessary that I
should forfeit my life for the furtherance
of the ends of justice and mingle my blood
with the blood of my children and with the
blood of millions in this slave country
whose rights are disregarded by wicked,
cruel and unjust enactments, I submit, so
let it be done.

Let me say one word further.

I feel entirely satisfied with the treatment
I have received on my trial, considering
all the circumstances, it has been more
generous than I expected, but I feel no
consciousness of guilt. I have stated from
the first what was my intention and what
was not. I never had any desire against
the life of any person or any disposition to
commit treason or general insurrection. I
never encouraged any man to do so, but

Here is where John Brown lived on Dr. Booth Kennedy's farm in Maryland, six miles from Harper's Ferry, at the time he made the attack on Harper's Ferry, Sunday night, October 16, 1859.

always discouraged any idea of the kind.

Let me say also a word in regard to the statement made by some of those connected with me. I hear it has been stated by some of them that I have induced them to join me, but the contrary is true. I do not say this to injure them, but as regretting their weakness, there is not one of them but what joined me of his own accord and expense, and the greater number of them I never saw and never had a word of conversation with, until the day they came to me and that was for the purpose I have stated.

"Now I have done."

In the hush that followed this quiet simple utterance, John Brown was sentenced to be hanged publicly on Friday, Dec. 2, 1859, between the hours of 9 A. M. and 4 P. M., the trap fell at 11:30 A. M.

Today, I can see him in my mind's eye as vividly as I saw him on the fateful day that he stood upon the scaffold, looking upon the earth for his last time. He was of sandy complexion, hair and beard thick and bushy, half gray; his height was over six feet, and weight about 185 pounds. He was 59 years, 5 months and 29 days old when he came to his death. He was a constant student of the Bible, reading it daily, and before his capture, it was his habit to have daily worship with his men. He never partook of a meal until he had asked the Divine blessing. His companion, Stevens, shown in the painting, was a very handsome man. He was 5 feet 10 inches high, weighed 190 pounds, had beautiful dark brown hair and beard, both of which were a little wavy. He presented a romantic picture on the day of execution. His hair and beard had been permitted to grow and his waxen complexion was a striking contrast. He wore a black broad cloth suit, a soft hat and a pair of boots, when hanged. The clothes were a gift of his sister. He was thirty-eight years of age.

As may well be supposed those were trying days in our little city. Governor Wise had made Charlestown his headquarters and had clothed the Harper's Ferry incident with national significance. The city was filled with soldiers 3,000 in all and among the people there was a rumor that the northern abolitionists were planning to swoop down upon the city and rescue the hero of the fight at the engine house. Forebodings of a coming storm were in the air, in everyone's heart and mind and mouths. Every natural phenomena was clothed with peculiar significance. The great comet that flamed across the heavens was taken as a sign of approaching war. Strange celestial lights, which nightly illuminated the heavens for weeks with a lurid brazen glow, the like of which had never been seen before by the people; filled their minds with morbid dread. Every one seemed on an intense strain. The slightest incident shattered the nerves. A few amusing things transpired which I will relate to give an idea of the popular feeling. At 11 o'clock Thursday night, November 10th, one of the pickets on the first line, stationed along the Winchester and Harper's Ferry railroad, became nervous and shot at a cow in Mr. Ranson's corn field. The shot caused great excitement. Word passed from mouth to mouth that an army of northern men were at the edge of town bent on rescuing John Brown. It caused intense excitement. The pickets were called in, the long roll was sounded by muffled drums, the shrill piping of fifes was heard, the rattle and clatter of arms and the tramp! tramp! of the soldiers disturbed the quiet of the night. Cannons were planted all around the jail, the soldiers formed a hollow square around the building and remained drawn up in line of battle until daylight. Again at 8 o'clock Sunday evening, November 20th, while a few of us youngsters were seated in the front parlor of the Savington house, which was then an immense barracks, we were startled by the noise of a drum falling to the floor. This was followed by the rattle of swords clashing together and of guns falling to the floor. They had been improperly hung and stacked against the folding doors of the back parlor. The awful din the articles made alarmed everyone. The Winchester Continentals had their headquarters in the back parlor and two other companies were billed in rooms on the second floor of the hotel. They all came rushing into the large hall, then valiantly made their way to the sidewalk. The Continentals were dressed in buckskin suits of the days of 1776, and the other companies in equally as picturesque raiment. Once outside the building the rumor gained currency that the

View of Harper's Ferry in 1859, showing the old wooden bridge of the Baltimore
& Ohio R. R. over the Potomac River. It
was also used for a wagon bridge. Here is
where John Brown crossed from the Maryland side with his twenty-two men Sunday
night, October 16, 1859, when he made the
attack on Harper's Ferry.

The above picture shows Hayward Shepherd sitting on his truck in his shirt sleeves. The old Negro that transferred baggage from the Baltimore & Ohio R. R. station over to the Winchester & Harper's Ferry R. R. station. He was killed by one of Brown's men just as they came off of the end of the bridge Sunday night, October 16th. It was contrary to Brown's orders; he told his men before they left the Kennedy farm to take no life except in self-defense.

northern men were at Cherry Run, preparing to attack the town.

Again the soldiers were mustered to the jail, cannons were planted so as to guard all approaches and the men kept in line of battle formation until daylight, and orders were given for no citizens to be on the streets within four blocks of the jail.

During those days the village of Charlestown was like a city besieged. No stranger was allowed to enter the town or depart without giving a strict account of him or herself. I remember that a gentleman from St. Louis was arrested and detained at the jail until he was identified and vouched for by an acquaintance, Joseph Easterday, a respectable citizen of Charlestown. He was then released and permitted to go on his way to Baltimore. Extraordinary precautions were taken on the day of the hanging of Brown. No stranger was allowed in the city and no citizen within the enclosure surrounding the scaffold.

He rose early that morning and continued writing until half past ten o'clock when he was told to prepare to die. He shook hands with the sheriff, visited the cell of Copeland and Green, and gave each a quarter of a dollar, saying he had no more use for money and bade them good bye. He next visited Cook and Coppoc the farmer he said had made a false confession. Said he had never sent Cook to Harper's Ferry as he had stated. He handed a quarter to them, shook hands and parted. He then gave a kindly good bye to his especial Comrade Stevens, gave him a quarter and told him not to betray his friends. Hazlett, the sixth one was confined in the same prison but he did not visit him, denying all knowledge of him. He walked out of the jail at 11 o'clock with a radiant countenance and the step of a conqueror, and it has been said that probably he had the lightest heart in Charlestown that day. He mounted the wagon which was a three seated spring wagon, taking the middle seat beside Sheriff Moore. Captain John Avis, the jailer and George Sadler the Undertaker sat on the front seat, and Deputy Jailer James Campbell occupied the back seat. The wagon was instantly surrounded by six companies of militia, cannons were so planted as to sweep every approach to the jail, and to blow the prisoner into atoms upon the first attempt of tumult.

Being asked on the way if he felt any fear, he replied: "It has been a characteristic of me from infancy not to suffer from physical fear. I have suffered a thousand times more from bashfulness than from fear." The day was clear and bright and he remarked as he rode that the country was beautiful and that they had some very fine residences, and when he got in sight of the militia in the field, he said, "You have quite a military display." Arriving at the gallows, he remarked, "I see no citizens here, where are they," "None but the troops are allowed to be present," was the reply. "That ought not to be," said he. "Citizens should be present as well as others." He then bade good bye to some acquaintances at the foot of the scaffold and was first to mount it. His step was still firm and his bearing calm, yet hopeful. The hour having come, he said to Captain Avis. "I have no words to thank you for all your kindness to me." How well I can remember that day. It was 11:30 o'clock on the forenoon of December 2, 1859. The execution took place on a scaffold situated on the top of a knoll in a ten acre field at the south edge of town. The soldiers were drawn up inside the inclosure, standing, with fixed bayonets, shoulder to shoulder. The military officers, Sheriff John Moore, Captain John Avis, the Jailer, and Deputy Jailer James Campbell, Dr. Strath the physician and George Saddler the undertaker were the only persons permitted to be near the scaffold. Two other boys and I stood on the roof of a lumber shed close by and witnessed the historic tragedy. I had in my possession my employer's field glasses and with the aid of these powerful lenses brought the principle actor in this awful drama as close to me as you are.

Brown stood on the scaffold facing the south, with his arms tied at the elbows and his legs tied at the ankles. He was asked if he had anything to say, but with an expression of weariness on his face he only responded: "No, I have nothing to say. I shall not detain you. Whenever you are ready, go ahead." Sheriff Moore then pulled the white cap over his face, placed the hangman's noose about his neck, adjusted the knot under the left ear. "He stood waiting for death," "Captain Brown" said the sheriff, "you are not standing on the drop, will you come forward." "I can't

Captain Albertis and party attack on John Brown in the old engine-house at Harper's Ferry, October 17, 1859, showing the Government's flag in the center of its grounds, and London Heights, Va., in he background.

see, was his firm answer; you must lead me." The sheriff led him forward to the center of the drop. "Shall I give you a handkerchief, and let you drop it as a signal?" "No, I am ready at any time, but do not keep me needlessly waiting." The sheriff then came down off the scaffold, took a hatchet and cut the rope, which ran down the right hand post from Brown. This tripped the trap on which he stood and the victim dropped with lightning quickness, the four and one-half feet which made the fall. His neck was instantly broken. He drew his legs up twice and turned facing the southeast, and when twenty minutes had transpired, Dr. Strath felt his pulse and pronounced him dead.

John Brown died as he lived tragically, bravely, as a lion to the last. His body was cut down and placed in the casket which George Saddler, the undertaker, had made for him from walnut. The casket was encased in a rough shipping box and hauled to the jail. At 4 o'clock the remains were conveyed to Harper's Ferry in a common lumber wagon where they were delivered to his widow, who conveyed them to his home, at North Elba, Essex County,

N. Y., where his bones lie mouldering in the grave, but his soul goes marching on.

Now gazing upon the second generation of men who have come upon the stage of the theatre of life since those dramatic days, I am one of very few, if any, living survivors, who witnessed the tragic scenes of those days. They were events that were big with meaning. I have treasured all the things which pertained to John Brown, because he was the one who fired the train which set the country ablaze for freedom of the slaves and the perpetuation of the union, and to show them to the children and children's children of those who enacted these scenes. This painting is true in every detail, a graphic picture of a tragic moment in the life of John Brown and the life of the nation—one that I hope will inspire patriotic emotions in the breasts of all who view it.

# CHAPTER II.

As before stated, John Brown was executed Dec. 2, 1859. Cook and Coppoc, two white men and Copeland and Green, two negroes, four of his men were executed December 16, fourteen days later. The two white men were hanged first. The scaffold not being large enough to hang all four at the same time, the two negroes stood close in the rear of the gallows, guarded by a large number of troops, and witnessed the awful tragedy which they were to perform in a few moments. Stevens and Hazlett were executed March 16, 1860, three months and fifteen days after Brown, making seven in all. They were all hanged in the same ten acre field and on the same scaffold, which was taken down each time and stored away in the jail yard, and was afterwards transformed into a portico in front of Mr. Rannels residence.

I roomed in a house directly across the street from the one possessing the historic portico and have in my possession a small piece of the lumber that was sawed off the end of the cross beam, from which **Brown** and his six men were hanged.

The right to remove the portico with an agreement to return it, was purchased by parties for more than the house it belonged to was worth. They had it at the Chicago World's Fair, as one of the exposition attractions. Also John Brown's fort, in which he was captured at Harper's Ferry, which was looked upon by thousands of people. It was also returned never to be removed again.

Cook and Hazlett were not taken prisoners at Harper's Ferry. They fled to Maryland early Monday morning, the 17th. Cook took position on the Maryland Heights with his sharps rifle and kept firing all day into Harper's Ferry at the Virginians, but so far as known no casualties resulted.

I remember hearing Mr. W. W. Burton, my employer, on his return home, telling and mimicing the report of Cook's gun and the sound of bullets therefrom. He said the report of Brown's guns were so different to that of the militia and citizens' guns.

Virginia offered two thousand dollars reward for the capture of Cook and Hazlett. **Cook** was caught the following week in

View of Harper's Ferry, Va., as it is to-day, showing the Potomac and Shenandoah Rivers. Also the Maryland Heights in Maryland to the left, and Louden Heights in Virginia to the right. The Shenandoah empties into the Potomac at the X. It shows the Baltimore & Ohio R. R. new iron bridge, and where the cars enter the tunnel. Just as they cross the Chesapeake and Ohio Canal on the Maryland side; it also shows the Blue Ridge Mountains in the distance, down the river.

Pennsylvania, not very far from Hagerstown, Maryland, and Hazlett was captured in the Pennsylvania mountains, about the 15th of November and turned over to the Virginia authorities. Mr. Syster of Hagerstown, Maryland, ex-sheriff of Washington county, Maryland, was the lucky winner of the two thousand dollars. Some of the Virginians disapproved of Gov. Wise having so many state troops at Charlestown, which put the state to an unnecessary heavy expense. He reviewed the troops every Wednesday afternoon, telling them the object of the North and what the slave states might expect.

I never failed to attend these drills. Wise was a good talker and as stated in my lecture a red hot secessionist. During the forty-six days of Brown's confinement at Charlestown, he received several visits from sympathizing Northern friends. Some of whom had never before seen him. No Virginian was known to give him any words of kindness, except the reverend clergy in the neighborhood, who tendered him the solace of religion after their fashion, which he civilly, but firmly declined. He could not recognize any one who justified or believed in slavery, as a minister of the God, he worshiped, or the Saviour in whom he trusted. To one of them who tryed to reconcile slavery, with christianity, he said. "My dear sir, you know nothing about christianity." You will have to learn the A. B. C's. in the lesson, as I find you are entirely ignorant of the meaning of the word. I of course respect you as a gentleman, but it is as a heathen gentleman. "Here the argument ended."

His wife overcoming many obstacles was finally permitted to visit him in his cell, and take supper with him a short time before his death. At the first of his confinement, he received a ciphered letter from one of his daughter's, which the authorities could not read. They got Miss Hunter, the state's attorney's daughter to read and interpret it for them, she being the only person in Charlestown that could read a secret writing. No one outside of the authorities ever knew what was in this letter. But the supposition was that they disapproved very much of its contents. Brown never got to see the letter and it was thought to be one cause of his wife having so much difficulty in gaining permission to visit him.

# CHAPTER III.

Many letters were addressed to Brown, while in prison and among them was one from Lydia Maria Child, who sought, but did not obtain permission from the Virginia authorities to visit him. Her letter was answered by Brown as follows:

"Mrs. L. Maria Child:

"My Dear Friend (such you prove to be, though a stranger) :—Your most kind letter has reached me, with the kind offer to come here and take care of me. Allow me to express my gratitude for your great sympathy, and at the same to propose to you a different course, together with my reasons for wishing it. I should certainly be greatly pleased to become personally acquainted with one so gifted and so kind; but I cannot avoid seeing some objections to it, under present circumstances. First, I am in charge of a most humane gentleman, who, with his family, have rendered me every possible attention I have desired, or that could be of the least advantage; and I am so far recovered from my wounds as no·

longer to require nursing. Then, again, it would subject you to great personal inconvenience and heavy expense, without doing me any good.

"Allow me to name to you another channel through which you may reach me with your sympathies much more effectually. I have at home a wife and three young daughters—the youngest but little over five years old, the oldest nearly sixteen. I have also two daughter-in-laws, whose husbands have both fallen near me here. There is also another widow, Mrs. Thompson, whose husband fell here. Whether she is a mother or not, I cannot say. All these, my wife included, live at North Elba, Essex County, New York. I have a middle-aged son, who has been in some degree, a cripple from childhood, who would have as much as he could well do to earn a living. He was a most dreadful sufferer in Kansas, and lost all he had laid up. He has not enough to clothe himself for the winter comfortably. I have no living son, or son-in-law, who did not suffer terribly in Kansas.

'Now, dear friend, would you not as soon contribute fifty cents now, and a like sum yearly, for the relief of those very poor and

The old government engine-house, now called John Brown's Fort, at Harper's Ferry, where he was captured Tuesday morning, October 18, 1859.

deeply afflicted persons, to enable them to supply themselves and their children with bread and very plain clothing and to enable the children to receive a common English education? Will you also devote your energies to induce others to join in giving a like amount, or any other amount, to constitute a little fund for the purpose named?

"I cannot see how your coming here can do me the least good, and I am quite certain you can do me immense good where you are. I am quite cheerful under all my afflicting circumstances and prospects; having as I humbly trust, 'the peace of God which passeth all understanding' to rule in my heart. You may make such use of this as you see fit. God Almighty bless and reward you a thousand fold!

"Yours in sincerity and truth,
"JOHN BROWN."

The following letter was written by Brown, while under sentence of death in answer to one he received from a relative residing in Wingham, Ohio:

"Charlestown, Jefferson Co., Va.,
19th Nov., 1859.

"Rev. Luther Humphrey,

"My Dear Friend: Your kind letter of

the 12th instant is now before me. So far as my knowledge goes as to our mutual kindred, I suppose I am the first since the landing of Peter Brown from the Mayflower that has either been sentenced to imprisonment or to the gallows. But, my dear old friend, let not that fact alone grieve you. You cannot have forgotten how and where our grandfather (Captain John Brown) fell in 1776, and that he, too, might have perished on the scaffold had circumstances been but very little different. The fact that a man dies under the hand of an executioner (or otherwise) has but little to do with his true character, as I suppose. John Rodgers perished at the stake, a great and good man, as I suppose; but his doing so does not prove that any other man that has died in the same way was good or otherwise. Whether I have any reason to be of good cheer (or not) in view of my end, I can assure you that I feel so; and that I am totally blinded if I do not really experience that strengthening and consolation you so faithfully implore in my behalf. The God of our Fathers reward your fidelity! I neither feel mortified, degraded, nor in the least ashamed of my imprisonment, my chain, or my near prospect of death by hanging. I feel assured 'that not one hair shall fall from my head without the will of my heavenly Father.' I also feel that I have long been endeavoring to hold exactly 'such a fast as God has chosen.' See the passage in Isaiah which you have quoted. No part of my life has been more happily spent than that I have spent here, and I humbly trust that no part has been spent to better purpose. I would not say this boastingly; but 'thanks be unto God who giveth us the victory,' through infinite grace.

"I should be 60 years old were I to live till May 9, 1860. I have enjoyed much of life as it is, and have been remarkably prosperous, having early learned to regard the welfare and prosperity of others as my own. I have never, since I can remember, required a great amount of sleep, so that I conclude that I have already enjoyed full an average number of waking hours with these who reach their 'three-score years and ten.' I have not as yet been driven to the use of glasses, but can see to read and write quite comfortably. But, more than that, I have generally enjoyed remarkably good health. I might go on to recount unnumbered and unmerited blessings, among which would be some very severe afflictions; and those the most needed blessings of all. And now, when I think how easily I might be left to spoil all I have done or suffered in the Cause of Freedom, I hardly dare wish another voyage, even if I had the opportunity. It is a long time since we met; but we shall now soon come together in our 'Father's house,' I trust. 'Let us hold fast that we already have,' remembering 'we shall reap in due time if we faint not.' Thanks be ever unto God, who giveth us the victory through Jesus Christ our Lord.' And now, my old warm-hearted friend, 'Good-bye,'

"Your affectionate cousin,

"JOHN BROWN."

Brown's letter written to his family, a week after his sentence to death:

"Charlestown, Jefferson Co. Va.,

"8th Nov. 1859.

"Dear Wife and Children:—Every one: I will begin by saying that I have in some degree recovered from my wounds, but that I am quite weak in my back, and sore about my left kidney. My appetite has been quite good for most of the time since I was hurt.

The old jail at Charlestown, Jefferson county, Virginia, where John Brown was imprisoned. The jailer lives in the front part.

The old Court House at Charlestown, Jefferson county, Virginia, where John Brown was tried. It stands diagonal across the street from the jail.

I am supplied with almost everything I could desire to make me comfortable, and the little I do lack (some articles of clothing, which I lost), I may perhaps soon get again. I am, besides, quite cheerful, having (as I trust) the peace of God, which 'passeth all understanding,' in some degree, of a good conscience that I have not lived altogether in vain. I can trust God with both the time and the manner of my death, believing, as I now do, that for me at this time to seal my testimony (for God and humanity) with my blood, will do vastly more toward advancing the Cause I have earnestly endeavored to promote than all I have done in my life before. I beg of you all meekly and quietly to submit to this; not feeling yourselves in the least degraded on that account. Remember, dear wife and children all, that Jesus of Nazareth suffered a most excruciating death on the Cross as a felon, under the most aggravating circumstances. Think, also, of the prophets, and apostles, and Christians of former days, who went through greater tribulations than you or I, and (try to) be reconciled. May God Almighty comfort all your hearts, and soon wipe away all tears from your eyes. To

Him be endless praise. Think, too, of the crushed millions who have no comforter. I charge you all never (in your trials) to forget the griefs of 'the poor that cry, and of those that have none to help them.' I write most earnestly to you my dear and afflicted wife not to come on, for the present at any rate. I will now give you my reasons for doing so. First, it would use up all the scanty means you have or at all likely to have, to make yourself and children comfortable hereafter. For let me tell you that the sympathy that is now around in your behalf may not always follow you. There is but little more of the romantic about helping poor widows and their children than there is about trying to relieve poor 'negroes.' Again, the little comfort it might afford us to meet again would be dearly bought by the pains of a final separation. We must part; and, I feel assured, for us to meet under such dreadful circumstances would only add to our distress. If you come on here, you must be only a gazing stock throughout the whole journey, to be remarked upon in every look, word, and act and by all sorts of creatures, and by all sorts of papers throughout the whole country. Again, it is my most decided judgment that in quietly and submissively staying at home, vastly more of generous sympathy will reach you, without such dreadful sacrifice of feeling as you, must put up with if you come on. The visits of one or two female friends that have come on here have produced great excitement, which is very annoying, and they cannot possibly do me any good. O Mary: do not come; but patiently wait for the meeting (of those who love God and their fellow-men) where no separation must follow. They shall go no more out forever. I greatly long to hear from some one of you, and to learn anything that in any way effects your welfare. I sent you ten dollars the other day. Did you get it? I have also endeavored to stir up Christian friends to visit and write to you in your deep affliction. I have no doubt that some of them, at least, will heed the call. Write to me, care of Capt. John Avis, Charlestown, Jefferson County, Va.

"Finally, my beloved, be of a good comfort.' May all your names be 'written in the Lamb's book of life'—may you all have the purifying and sustaining influence of the Christian religion—is the earnest prayer of your affectionate husband and father.

"JOHN BROWN."

"P. S. I cannot remember a night so dark as to have hindered the coming day, nor a storm so furious or dreadful as to prevent the return of warm sunshine and a cloudless sky. But, beloved ones, do remember that this is not your rest, that in this world you have no abiding-place or continuing city. To God and His infinite mercy I always commend you.     J. B."

"Nov. 9."

John Brown on the way to be executed two and one-half blocks from the jail to his scaffold.

# CHAPTER IV.

October 17, 1859, this country was bewildered and astounded, while the slave states were convulsed with fear and rage, by telegraph dispatches from Baltimore, announcing the outbreak at Harper's Ferry.

Here follows the dispatches which gave the first tidings:

"INSURRECTION AT HARPER'S FERRY."
"To the Associated Press:

"Baltimore, Monday, Oct. 17, 1859.

"A dispatch just received here from Frederick, and dated this morning, states that an insurrection has broken out at Harper's Ferry, where an armed band of Abolitionists have full possession of the Government Arsenal. The express train going east was twice fired into, and one of the railroad hands and a negro killed, while they were endeavoring to get the train through the town. The insurrectionists stopped and arrested two men, who had come to town with a load of wheat, and, seizing their wagons, loaded them with rifles, and sent them into Maryland.

The insurrectionists number about 250 whites, and are aided by a gang of negroes. At last accounts, fighting was going on.

"The above is given just as it was received here. It seems very improbable, and should be received with great caution, until affirmed by further advices. A later dispatch, received at the railroad office, says the affair has been greatly exaggerated. The reports had their foundation in a difficulty at the Armory, with which negroes had nothing to do.

"Baltimore, 10 o'clock.

'It is apprehended that the affair at Harper's Ferry is more serious than our citizens seem willing to believe. The wires from Harper's Ferry are cut, and consequently we have no telegraphic communications with Monocacy Station. The southern train which was due here at an early hour this morning has not yet arrived. It is rumored that there is a stampede of negroes from this State. There are many other wild rumors, but nothing authentic as yet.

"Baltimore, Monday, Oct. 17.—2 P. M.

"Another account received by train says the bridge across the Potomac was filled with insurgents all armed. Every light in the town was extinguished, and the hotels closed. All the streets were in the possession of the mob, and every road and lane leading thereto barricaded and guarded. Men were seen in every quarter with muskets and bayonets, who arrested the citizens and impressed them into the service, including many negroes. This done, the United States Arsenal and Government Pay-house, in which was said to be a large amount of money, and all other public works, were seized by the mob. Some were of the opinion that the object was entirely plunder and to rob the Government of the funds deposited on Saturday at the Pay-house. During the night, the mob made a demand on the Wager Hotel for provisions and enforced the claim by a body of armed men. The citizens were in a terrible state of alarm, and the insurgents have threatened to burn the town.

"The following has just been received from Monocacy, this side of Harper's Ferry:

"The Mail Agent on the western-bound train has returned and reports that the train was unable to get through. The town is in possession of the negroes, who arrest everyone they can catch and imprison. The train due here at 3 P. M. could not get through, and the Agent came down down on an empty engine."

Probably the more prevalent sensation at first was caused by Harper's Ferry being the seat of a National Armory, at which a large number of mechanics and artisans were usually employed by the Government, it was supposed by many that some collision respecting wages or hours of labor had occurred between the officers and the workmen, which had provoked a popular tumult, and perhaps a stoppage of the trains passing through that village on the Baltimore & Ohio Railroad; and that this, magnified by rumor and alarm, has afforded a basis for these monstrous exaggerations. Yet, as time wore on, further advices, with particulars and circumstances, left no room to doubt the substantial truth of the original report. An attempt had actually been made to excite a slave insurrection in Northern Virginia, and the one man in America to whom such an enterprise would not seem utter insanity and suicide, was at the head of it.

The X on the above picture marks the
exact spot where John Brown's scaffold
stood when he was executed, December 2,
1859. At that time it was in the center of
a ten-acre field at the south edge of the
town, but since then it has been built up
with fine buildings, and is now the finest
residence portion of Charlestown. Col.
John Gibson, a Confederate Colonel, an old
resident of Charlestown, purchased this
spot of ground and erected his fine residence here, as you see.

# CHAPTER V.

## THE BROWN FAMILY.

John Brown was sixth in descent from Peter Brown, a carpenter by trade and a Puritan of intense conviction, who was one of the glorious company who came over in the Mayflower, and landed at Plymouth Rock, on that memorable 22nd of December, 1620. The fourth in descent from Peter the pilgrim was John Brown, born in 1728, who was captain of the West Simsbury (Connecticut) trainband, and in that capacity joined the Continental Army at New York in the spring of 1776, and, after two months' service, fell a victim to camp-fever, dying in a barn a few miles north of the city. His grandson, John Brown, of Osawatomie, Kan., son of Owen and Ruth Brown, was born in Torrington, Conn., May 9, 1800. On his mother's side, he was descended from Peter Miles, an emigrant from Holland, who settled at Bloomfield, Conn., about 1700; and his grandfather on this side, Gideon Miles, also served in the Revolutionary War, and attained the rank of lieutenant.

When John was but five years old, his father migrated to Hudson, Ohio, where he died a few years later, aged eighty-seven. He was engaged, during the last war, in furnishing beef cattle to our force on the northern frontier; and his son, John, then twelve years of age, accompanied him as a cattle-driver, and in that capacity witnessed Hull's surrender at Detroit in 1812. He was so disgusted with what he saw of military life that he utterly refused, when of suitable age, to train or drill in the militia, but paid fines or evaded service during his entire liability to military duty. In an auto-biographical fragment, written by him in 1857, for a child who had evinced a deep interest in his Kansas efforts, speaking of himself in the third person, he says:

"During the war with England, a circumstance occurred that in the end made him a most determined Abolitionist, and led him to declare, or swear, eternal war with Slavery. He was staying, for a short time, with a very gentlemanly landlord, once a United States Marshal, who held a slave-boy near his own age, active, intelligent, and good-feeling, and to whom John was under considerable obligation for numerous little acts of kindness. The master made a great pet of John, brought him to table with his first company and friends called their attention to every little smart thing he said or did, and to the fact of his being more than a hundred miles from home with a drove of cattle alone; while the negro boy (who was fully, if not more than, his equal), was badly clothed, poorly fed and lodged in cold weather, and beaten before his eyes with iron shovels, or any other thing that came first to hand. This brought John to reflect on the wretched, hopeless condition of fatherless and motherless-slave children: for such children have neither fathers nor mothers to protect and provide for them. He sometimes would raise the question, is God their Father?"

Young John had very little of what is called education; poverty and hard work being his principal teachers. At sixteen years of age, he joined the Congregational Church in Hudson; and from fifteen to twenty he learned the trade of tanner and currier. He returned to New England while still a minor, and commenced, at Plainfield, Mass., a course of study with a view to the Christian ministry; but, being attacked with inflammation of the eyes, which ultimately became chronic, he relinquished this pursuit and returned to Ohio, where he married his first wife, Dianthe Lusk, when a little more than twenty years of age. By her, he had seven children, the last of whom, born in 1832, was buried with her three days after its birth. He next year married Mary A. Day (who survives him), by whom he had thirteen children, of whom three sons were with him at Harper's Ferry, two of whom lost their lives there, and the third escaped. Eight of his children were living at the time of his death.

Mr. Rannell's residence at Charlestown, Virginia, showing the portico that is built out of John Brown's scaffold.

# CHAPTER VI.

## OCCUPATION.

Brown worked for himself as a tanner and farmer five or six years in northern Ohio, and for nine years thereafter in Crawford county, Pennsylvania, enjoying general respect as a sincere, earnest, upright, pious man. One who knew him in those days remembers that the wrong of Slavery was a favorite topic with him, Though stern in manner, he was often affected to tears when depicting the unmerited sufferings of slaves. So early as 1839, the idea of becoming himself a liberator of the unhappy race was cherished by him. From 1835 to 1846, he lived once more in northern Ohio, removing thence to Springfield, Mass., where he engaged in wool-dealing under the firm name of Perkins & Brown, selling wool extensively on commission for growers along the southern shore of Lake Erie, and undertaking to dictate prices and a system of grading wools to the manufactures of New England, with whom he came to an open rupture, which induced him at length to ship two hundred thousand pounds of wool to London, and go thither to sell it. This bold experiment proved a failure, wool bringing far higher prices in this country than in any other. He finally sold at a fearful loss and came home a bankrupt. But, meantime, he had traveled considerably over Europe and learned something of the ways of the world.

In 1849 he removed with his family to North Elba, Essex county, New York, to some land given him by our noblest philanthropist, Gerrit Smith. The location was a hard one, high up among the glens of the Adirondack Mountains, rugged, cold and bleak. The negroes generally became discouraged, in view of the incessant toil, privation, and hardships, involved in hewing a farm and a habitation out of the primitive wilderness, in a secluded, sterile region, and gave over in despair after a brief trial; but John Brown and his sons persevered, ultimately making homes for themselves, which though not luxurious nor inviting, their families retain. In 1851, the father returned with his family to Akron, Ohio, where he once more carried on the wool business and managed the farm of a friend; but, in 1855, on starting for Kansas, he moved his famıly back to their own home at North Elba, where they remain, with his grave in their midst.

## CHAPTER VII.

### BLEEDING KANSAS.

In 1854 his four elder sons — all by his first wife, and all living in Ohio — determined to migrate to Kansas. They went thither, primarily, to make that a Free State; secondly, to make homes for themselves and their families. They went unarmed, having a very inadequate idea of the nature and spirit of the fiend they were defying. They settled in Lykins county, southern Kansas, about eight miles distant from the present village of Osawatomie, and not far from the Missouri border. Here they were soon so harrassed, threatened, insulted and plundered by gangs of marauding ruffians from Missouri, that they found it impossible to remain without arms, and they wrote to their father to produce such as they needed. He obtained them; and, to make sure work of it, went with them.

Nearly all others went to Kansas in the hope of thereby improving their worldly condition, or, at least, of making homes there. John Brown went there for the sole purpose of fighting, if need be, for liberty. He left his family behind, for he had no intention of making Kansas his home. He was no politician, in the current acceptation of the term, having taken little or no interest in party contests for many years.

Of course, he was not pleased with what he found and saw in Kansas. There were too much policy, too much politics, and too general a regard for personal safety and comfort. He would have preferred a good deal less riding about, especially at night, with more solid fighting. Redpath, who visited him in his camp near Prairie City, not long before the battle of Black Jack, says:

"I shall not soon forget the scene that there opened to my view. Near the edge of the creek, a dozen horses were tied, all ready saddled for a ride for life, or a hunt after Southern invaders. A dozen rifles and sabres were stacked around the trees. In an open space, amid the shady and lofty woods, there was a great blazing fire with

Lawson Botts, John Brown's defendant in the justice court, assisted by C. J. Faulkner, and in the circuit court he had Botts and L. C. Green; he dismissed these and took on George H. Hoyt, of Boston, who volunteered his services.

George H. Hoyt, the boy lawyer from Boston, as the Virginians call him. John Brown's attorney, assisted by Samuel Chilton, of Washington, D. C., and Hiram Griswold, of Cleveland, Ohio, who addressed the jurors with great force and discretion.

a pot on it; a woman, bare-headed, with an honest sun-burnt face, was picking black-berries from the bushes; three or four armed men were lying on red and blue blankets on the grass; and two fine-looking youths were standing, leaning on their arms, on guard, near by. One of them was the youngest son of Old Brown, and the other was 'Charley,' the brave Hungarian, who was subsequently murdered at Osawa-tomie. Old Brown himself stood near the fire, with his shirt-sleeves rolled up, and a large piece of pork in his hand. He was cooking a pig. He was poorly clad, and his toes protruded from his boots. The old man received me with great cordiality, and the little band gathered about me. But it was for a moment only; for the Captain ordered them to renew their work. He respectfully, but firmly, forbade conversa-tion on the Pottawatomie; and said that, if I desired any information from the com-pany in relation to their conduct or in-tentions, he as their Captain, would an-swer for them whatever it was proper to communicate.

"In this camp, no manner of profane lan-guage was permitted; no man of immoral character was allowed to stay, except as a prisoner of war. He made prayers, in which all the company united, every morning and evening; and no food was ever tasted by his men until the Divine blessing had been asked on it. After every meal, thanks were returned to the Bountiful Giver. Often, I was told, the old man would retire to the densest solitudes to wrestle with his God in secret prayer. One of his company subsequently informed me that, after these retirings, he would say that the Lord had directed him in visions what to do; that, for himself, he did not love warfare, but peace — only acting in obedience in the will of the Lord, and fighting God's battles for His children's sake.

"It was at this time that the old man said to me: I would rather have the small-pox, yellow fever, and cholera all together in my camp, than a man without principles. It's a mistake, sir, he continued, that our people make, when they think that bullies are the best fighters or that they are the men fit to oppose these Southerners. Give me men of good principles — God-fearing men, men who respect themselves —and, with a dozen of them, I will oppose any hundred such men as these Buford ruffians."

"I remained in the camp about two hours. Never before had I met such a band of men. They were not earnest, but earnestness incarnate. Six of them were John Brown's sons."

In the August following, a new invasion, on an extensive scale, of Kansas, from the Missouri border, was planned and executed. Inflammatory proclamations were issued, which affirmed that the pro-Slavery settlers either had been or were about to be killed or driven out of the Territory by the Abolitionists, and the Missourians were exhorted to rally all their forces for the conflict. Lexington, Mo., was assigned as the place, and August 20th as the time of assemblage, for LaFayette county, and New Santa Fe, Jackskon county, as the general rendezvous. "Bring your guns, your horses, and your clothing, all ready to go on to Kansas: our motto will be this time 'No Quarter.' Let no one stay away!" A similar appeal was issued from Westport, signed by Atchison, Springfellow, and others. A force of two thousand men was by virtue of these appeals collected at the petty village of Santa Fe, directly on the border; but soon divided into two expeditions, one of which, led by Senator Atchison, was confronted at Bull Creek by not more than half its number under Gen. J. H. Lane, and turned back without a fight—first halting, and refusing to advance against the determined front of the Free-State men, and finally disappearing in the course of the ensuing night. The other and smaller party, led by Gen. Reid, consisted of four to five hundred men, well armed with the United States cannon, muskets, bayonets, and revolvers, and liberally supplied with ammunition. They pursued a more southerly course, and, at daylight on the morning of August 30th, approached the little village of Osawatomie, which was defended by barely forty-one Free-State men; but their leader was old John Brown. His son Frederick was shot dead, about a mile and a half from the village by the Rev. Martin White, who led the pro-Slavery advance or scouting party, before young Brown was aware of their hostile character. Two other Free-State men were likewise surprised and killed early in the morning.

John Brown, with his forty-one compatriots, took position in great haste in the

Andrew Hunter, prosecutor in John Brown's trial. He was one of Virginia's ablest attorneys at that time.

timber on the southern bank of the little river Osage, here known as the Marais-des-Cygnes, a little to the northwest of the village, and here fought the advance of the foe as they approached, until thirty-one or two of them were killed and from forty to fifty wounded. The Free-State men, fighting generally under cover against an undisciplined and badly managed force, lost but five or six in all; but the disproportion was too great, and, their ammunition becoming exhausted, they were forced to retreat, leaving Osawatomie to be sacked and burned again. Brown himself continued steadily firing, as well as directing his men, throughout the conflict, amid an incessant shower of grapeshot and bullets. Not until he saw the whites of the enemy's eyes did he give the order to his little band to retreat. The Ruffians killed the only wounded prisoner whom they took, as also a Mr. Williams, whom they found in Osawatomie, and who had taken no part in the conflict. The Missourians returned to their homes in triumph, boasting that they had killed old Brown and dispersed his band; but their wagon-loads of dead and wounded created a salutary awe, which was very efficient in preventing future invasions, or rendering them comparatively infrequent.

The Rev. Martin White, for his services in this expedition, was chosen a member of the next Lecompton (pro-Slavery) Legislature, which he attended; and, in the course of its deliberations, he entertained his fellow-members with a graphic and humorous account of his killing of Frederick Brown. When the session was finished, he started for home, but never reached it. His body was found cold and stiff on the prairie, with a rifle-ball through his votals.

Six weeks after the Osawatomie fight, Capt. Brown was in Lawrence, stopping over Sunday on his way home from Topeka, when the startling announcement was made that 2,800 Missourians, under Atchison and Reid, were advancing upon that town. Not more than two hundred men in all could be rallied for its defense. Brown was unanimously chosen their leader. He made a speech from a dry-goods box in Main street, opposite the post-office, substantially as follows:

"Gentlemen, it is said there are twenty-five hundred Missourians down at Franklin, and that they will be here in two hours. You can see for yourselves the smoke they are making by setting fire to the houses in that town. Now is probably the last opportunity you will have of seeing a fight; so that you had better do your best. If they should come up and attack us, don't yell and make a great noise, but remain perfectly silent and still. Wait till they get within twenty-five yards of you; get a good object; be sure you see the hindsight of your gun; then fire. A great deal of powder and lead, and very precious times, are wasted by shooting too high. You had better aim at their legs than at their heads. In either case, be sure of the hind sights of your guns. It is from this reason that I myself have so many times escaped; for, if all the bullets which have been aimed at me had hit me, I should have been as full of holes as a riddle."

He proceeded to post his men so admirably as to conceal entirely their paucity of numbers, taking advantage of a gentle ridge, running east and west, at some distance south of the town. The hostile forces remained through the night about half a mile from each other, with a corn-field be-

tween, each man covered by the grass and
the inequalities of the ground, their posi-
tions only revealed by the flashes and reports of their guns. When the sun rose
next morning, the Missourians had decamped.

Capt. Brown left soon after for the East
by the circuitous land route through Nebraska and Iowa; that through Missouri
being closed against Free-State men. He
took a fugitive slave in his wagon and saw
him safely on his way to freedom. He made
two or three visits to the East in quest of
aid and of funds, returning for the last
time to Southern Kansas in the Autumn
of 1858. Peace had finelly been secured in
all that part of the Territory lying north of
the Kansas river, by the greatly increased
numbers and immense preponderance of the
Free-State settlers, rendering raids from
Missouri, whether to carry elections or de-
vastate settlements, too perilous to be light-
ly undertaken. When the Missourians
still rallied, in obedience to habit, at Kansas elections, they did so at Oxford, Santa
Fe, and other polls held just along the border, when they could suddenly concentrate
force enough to make the operation a tol-

## JOHN BROWN'S GRAVE.

John Brown's grave at North Elba, Essex county, New York. This tombstone was his grandfather's, Capt. John Brown, who died in the War of 1776 in a barn near New York City and was buried at Torrington, Conn., and while John Brown lived at North Elba, he went to Connecticut and helped to put a monument at his grandfather's grave, and when he came home he brought this stone with him. And just before he started for Harper's Ferry, he left a request with the Sexton of North Elba Cemetery,

Alonzo Washburn, and with his family, who stayed at home, that if he should die in the near future, he wished to be brought back home and buried at this point, with his feet toward the two letters "J. B." that he cut in the large rock himself, considering this big rock to be his monument, and to have this stone that stood at his grandfather's grave set at the head of his, and such additional inscription on it as were necessary, just below that of his grandfather's, which reads as follows: "In memory of Capt. John Brown, who died at New York, Sept. 3, 1776, in the forty-eighth year of his age."

John Brown, born May 9, 1800, was executed at Charlestown, Virginia, December 2, 1859.

Oliver Brown, killed at Harper's Ferry, Oct. 17, 1859.

Watson Brown, wounded at Harper's Ferry, Oct. 17, 1859, and died Oct. 18, 1859.

Watson is buried next to his father, John Brown, and Oliver is buried in the third grave and eight others with him. Hazlett and Stevens were taken up and brought here, and put together in one new casket and buried in the same grave. Four more of Brown's men were killed at Harper's Ferry, three of them being buried at Harper's Ferry. The fourth one tried to escape by wading the Potomac and was killed under the bridge; when about the middle of the river, by Willes King, a shoemaker, from Charlestown, Virginia. He floated down the river and so far as known was never taken out.

Five of John Brown's children are still living, one son near Putin Bay, Ohio, and one son and three daughters in Pasedena, California.

erably safe one.  But Southern Kansas was
still very thinly settled, in part by Missourians; while Fort Scott, a military post and
land-office in the heart of that section, afforded a nucleus and rallying-point for pro-
Slavery terrorism.  The Missourians, rec-
ognizing and acting under the Territorial
Legislature and local officers created by the
Border Ruffian irruptions and fraudulent
elections, claimed to be the party of Law
and Order, and often, if not usually com-
mitted their outrages under the lead of a
marshal or a sheriff.  The Free-State men,
repudiating and scouting those elections
and their fruits, were regarded and treated,
not only by the pro-Slavery party on either
side of the border, but by the Federal Ad-
ministration and its instruments in Kansas,
outlaws and criminals.  At length, Fort
Scott itself was captured by Montgomery,
one of the boldest of the Free-State leaders,
who, with 150 men, entered it by night,
made temporary prisoners of its dignita-
ries, and liberated a Free-State man imprisoned there.  Montgomery soon after
surrendered himself to the Federal Governor of the Territory, when a treaty or understanding was had between them, under

which the region gradually settled into com-
parative peace.

But, while the ferment was at its height,
and forces were gathering on both sides for
the conflict, a slave named Jim came secret-
ly across the border to Capt. Brown's cab-
in, and told him that himself and his family
had been sold, and were to be sent off to
Texas next day. Brown, with twenty men,
divided into two parties, crossed the border
in the night, liberated Jim and his family,
and, proceeding to the house of another
slave-holder, gave deliverance to five more
slaves. The other party, under Kagi, called
at several houses in search of slaves, but
found none until they reached the residence
of David Cruse, who, learning their object,
seized his rifle and raised it to fire, but was
instantly shot dead. He had but one slave,
who accompanied his liberators on their retreat. One of the captured slaveholders
was carried several miles into the Territory
to prevent his raising a hue-and-cry for
rescue.

A furious excitement throughout Western Missouri inevitably followed. The
Governor offered a reward of three thousand dollars for the arrest of Brown, on

his part; to which President Buchanan added two hundred and fifty dollars. It was reported that the slave population of the two adjacent Missouri counties was diminished from five hundred to fifty within a few weeks, mainly by removal for sale.

Brown was resolved to leave Kansas, and started early in January, 1859, passing through Lawrence on his northward route. He had four white companions, three of whom afterward fought under him at Harper's Ferry, and three negroes, besides women and children. He was pursued by thirty pro-Slavery men from Lecompton so sharply that he was compelled to halt and prepare for a defense. He took possession of two deserted log-cabins in the wilderness, which his pursuers surrounded, at a respectful distance, and sent to Atchison and Lecompton for reinforcements. From Atchison, twelve men arrived, making their force forty-two to his eight. As they were preparing to attack, Brown and his seven companions suddenly issued from the wood, in order of battle, when the valorous posse turned and fled. Not a shot was fired, as they, putting spurs to their horses, galloped headlong across the prairie,

Judge Richard Parker, who presided at John Brown's trial.

and were soon lost to vview. Only four
men stood their ground, and these were
made prisoners forthwith. Brown ordered
them to dismount, and give their horses to
his negroes. This command occasioned—
not to say provoked—profane language on
their part; whereupon he commanded silence, saying he would permit no blasphemy
in his presence. At this, they only swore
the louder and harder. "Kneel!" exclaimed
the stern Puritan, suddenly presenting his
pistol. There was no alternative but a dead-
ly one, and they all knelt. "Now pray!"
It was probably their first attempt in that
line for many years, and their success could
hardly have been brilliant; but he kept
them at it until they had at least manifested
an obedient and docile spirit. They never
swore again in his presence, though he held
them prisoners for five days, compelling
them, each and all, to pray night and morning. These four were from Atchison; and,
being finally liberated, returned to that pro-
Slavery city, where one of them was green
enough to tell the story of their capture,
and their discipline under old John Brown.
The laugh was so general and so hearty
that they soon left, never to return.

Brown was joined, soon after this "Battle of the Spurs," by Kagi, with forty mounted men from Topeka, of whom seventeen escorted him safely to Nebraska City. He there crossed the Missouri into Iowa, and traveled slowly through that State, Illinois, and Michigan, to Detroit, where he arrived on the 12th of March, crossing mmediately into Canada, with his twelve blacks—one of them born since he left Missouri—were legally, as well as practically, free. All of them were industrious, prosperous, and happy, when last heard many months thereafter.

Brown returned to the States soon after his triumphal entry into Canada as a liberator, and was at Cleveland, Ohio, from the 20th to the 30th of March. He entered his name on the hotel book as "John Brown, of Kansas," advertised two horses for sale at auction; and, at the time of the sale, stood in front of the auctioneer's stand, notifying all bidders that the title might be considered defective, since he had taken the horses with the slaves whom he liberated in Western Missouri, finding it necessary to his success that the slaves should have horses, and that the masters should not. "But," he added, when telling the story afterward, "they brought a very excellent price."

## CHAPTER VIII.

### PLANNING THE RAID ON HARPER'S FERRY.

Early in April following, he was in Ashtabula county, Ohio, sick of the ague. He visited his family in Essex county, New York, toward the end of that month. In May, he was in New York City, Rochester, and Boston, where he learned to manufacture crackers. On the 3rd of June, he was at Collinville, Conn., where he closed a contract for a thousand pikes, that he had ordered some time before.

He was soon afterward again in Northern Ohio, and in Western Pennsylvania, proceeding by Pittsburg and Bedford to Chambersburg, where he remained several days. He was in Hagerstown, Md., on the 30th, where he registered his name as "Smith, and two sons, from New York." He told his landlord that they had been farming in Western New York, but had been discouraged by losing two or three

years' crops by frost, and they were now
looking for a milder climate, in a locality
adapted to wool-growing, etc. After looking about Harper's Ferry for several days,
they found six miles from that village a
large farm, with three unoccupied houses,
the owner, Dr. Booth Kennedy, having died
the last Spring. These houses they rented
for a trifle until the next March, paying the
rent in advance, purchasing for cash a lot
of hogs from the family, and agreeing to
take care of the stock on the farm until it
could be sold, which they faithfully did.
After they had lived there a few weeks,
attracting no observation, others joined
them from time to time, including two of
Brown's young daughters; and one would
go and another come, without exciting any
particular remark. They paid cash for everything, were sociable and friendly with
their neighbors, and seemed to pass their
time mainly hunting in the mountains;
though it was afterward remembered that
they never brought home any game. On
one occasion, a neighbor remarked to the
elder Mr. Smith (as old Brown was called)
that he had observed twigs and branches
bent down in a peculiar maner; which

Captain John Avis, John Brown's jailer.

John Brown's monument at Ossawatomie, Kansas, where he stood on a low hill, west of the town, with forty-one armed men, August 30, 1856, and fought four hundred Border Ruffians, making a terrific and bloody battle. It is here that Brown lost his son Frederick.

Smith explained by stating that it was the habit of Indians, in traveling through a strange country, to mark their path thus, so as to be able to find their way back. He had no doubt, he said, that Indians passed over these mountains, unknown to the inhabitants.

Meantime, the greater number of the men kept out of sight during the day, so as not to attract attention, while their arms, ammunitions, etc., were being gradually brought from Chambersburg, in well-secured boxes. No meal was eaten on the farm, while old Brown was there, until a blessing had been asked upon it; and his Bible was in daily requisiton.

The night of the 24th of October was originally fixed upon by Brown for the first blow against Slavery in Virginia, by the capture of the Federal Arsenal at Harper's Ferry; and his biographer, Redpath, alleges that many were on their way to be with him on that occasion, when they were paralyzed by the intelligence that the blow had already been struck, and had failed. The reason given for this, by one who was in his confidence, is, that Brown, who had been absent, on a secret journey to the North, suspected that one of his party was a traitor, and that he must strike prematurely, or not at all. But the woman who had been with them at the Kennedy farm—the wives or daughters of one or another of the party—had already been quietly sent away; and the singular complexion of their household had undoubtedly begun to excite curiosity, if not alarm, among their neighbors. On Saturday, the 15th, a council was held, and a plan of operations discussed. On Sunday evening another council was held, and the programme of the chief unanimously approved.

He closed it with these words:

"And now, gentlemen, let me press this one thing on your minds. You all know how dear life is to you, and how dear your lives are to your friends; and, in remembering that, consider that the lives of others are as dear to them as yours are to you. Do not, therefore, take the life of any one if you can possibly avoid it; but, if necessary to take life in order to save your own, then make sure work of it."

# CHAPTER IX.

Harper's Ferry was then a village of some five thousand inhabitants, lying on the Virginia side of the Potomac, and on either side of its principal tributary, the Shenandoah, which here enters it from the Southwest. Its site is a mere nest or cup among high, steep mountains; the passage of the united rivers through the Blue Ridge at this point having been pronounced by Thomas Jefferson a spectacle which one might well cross the Atlantic to witness and enjoy. Here the Baltimore & Ohio Railroad crosses the Potomac; and the rich valley of the Shenandoah is traversed for a considerable distance hence by the Winchester and Harper's Ferry Railroad. Washington is fifty-seven miles distant by turnpike; Baltimore, eighty miles by railroad. Modest as the village then was, space had been with difficulty found for its habitations, some of which were perched upon ground four hundred feet above the surface of the streams. One of its very few streets was entirely occupied by the work shops and offices of the National Armory, and had an iron railing across its entrance. In the old Arsonal building, there were usually stored from 100,000 to 200,000 stand of arms. The knowledge of this had doubtless determined the point of which the first blow of the liberators was to be struck.

## CHAPTER X.

### THE ASSAULT ON HARPER'S FERRY.

The forces with which Brown made his attack consisted of seventeen white and five colored men, though it is said that others who escaped assisted outside, by cutting the telegraph wires and tearing up the railroad track. The entrance of this petty army into Harper's Ferry on Sunday evening, October 16, seems to have been effected without creating alarm. They first rapidly extinguished the lights of the town; then took possession of the Armory building, which were only guarded by three watchmen, whom, without meeting resistance or exciting alarm, they seized and locked up in the guard-house. It is probable that they

John Brown, as he looked in 1857.

were aided, or, at least, guided, by friendly negroes belonging in the village. At half-past ten, the watchman at the Potomac bridge was seized and secured. At midnight, his successor, arriving, was hailed by Brown's sentinels, but ran, one shot being fired at him from the bridge. He gave the alarm, but slitl nothing stirred. At a quarter-past one, the western train arrived, and its conductor found the bridge guarded by armed men. He and others attempted to walk across, but were turend back by presented rifles. One man, a negro, was shot in the back, and died next morning. The passengers took refuge in the hotel, and remained there several hours; the conductor properly refusing to pass the train over, though permitted, at three o'clock to do so.

A little after midnight, the house of Col. Washington was visited by six of Brown's men under Capt. Stevens, who captured the Colonel, seized his arms, and liberated his slaves. On their return, Stevens and party visited the house of Mr. Alstadtt and his son, whom they captured and freed their slaves. These, with each male citizen as he appeared in the street, were confined in the Armory until they numbered between forty and fifty. Brown informed his prisoners that they could be liberated on condition of writing to their friends to send a negro apiece as ransom. At daylight the train proceeded, Brown walking over the bridge with the conductor. Whenever any one asked the object of their captors, the uniform answer was, "To free the slaves;" and when one of the workmen, seeing an armed guard at the Arsenal gate, asked by what authority they had taken possession of the public property, he was answered, "By the authority of God Almighty!"

The passenger train that sped eastward from Harper's Ferry, by Brown's permission, in the early morning of Monday, October 17th, left that place completely in the military possession of the insurrectionists. They held, without dispute, the Arsenal, with its offices, workshops, and grounds. Their sentinels stood on guard at the bridges and principal corners, and were seen walking up and down the streets. Every workingman, who ignorantly approached the Armory, as day dawned, was seized and imprisoned, with all other white males who seemed capable of making any trouble. By eight o'clock the number of prisoners had been swelled to sixty-odd, and the work was still proceeding.

But it was no longer entirely one-sided. The white Virginians, who had arms, and who remained unmolested in their houses, prepared to use them. Soon after daybreak, as Brown's guards were bringing two citizens to a halt, they were fired on by a man named Turner, and directly afterward, by a grocer named Boerly, who was instantly killed by the return fire. Several Virginians soon obtained possession of a room overlooking the Armory gates, and fired thence at the sentinels who guarded them, one of whom fell dead, and another —Brown's son, Watson—was mortally wounded. Still, throughout the forenoon, the liberators remained masters of the town. There were shots fired from one side or the other at intervals, but no more casualties reported. The prisoners were by turns permitted to visit their families under guard, to give assurance that they still lived and were kindly treated. Had Brown chosen to fly to the mountains with his few followers, he might still have done so, though with a much slendered chance of impunity than if he had, according to his original plan, decamped at midnight, with such arms and ammunition as he could bear away. Why he lingered, to brave inevitable destruction, is not certain; but it may fairly be presumed that he had private assurances that the negroes of the surrounding country would rise at the first tidings of his movement and come flocking to his standard; and he chose to court the desperate chances of remaining where arms and ammunition for all could be abundantly had. True, he afterward said that he had arms enough already, either on or about his premises; but, if so, why seize Harper's Ferry?

## CHAPTER XI.

### CAPTURE AND EXECUTION OF BROWN AND HIS COMRADES.

At all events, if his doom was already sealed, his delay at least hastened it. Half an hour after noon, a militia force, four hundred strong, arrived from Charleston, the county seat, and were rapidly disposed so as to command every available exit from

John Brown's Fort as it stands today, up the Shenandoah River at Harper's Ferry, after its return from the Chicago World's Fair. It is never to be removed again.

the place. In taking the Shenandoah bridge, they killed one of the insurgents, and captured William Thompson, a neighbor of Brown's, at Elba, unwounded. The rifle-works were next attacked, and speedily carried, being defended by five insurgents only. These attempted to cross the river and four of them succeeded in reaching a rock in the middle of it, whence they fought with four hundred Virginians, who lined either bank, until two of them were dead, and a third mortally wounded, when the fourth surrendered. Kagi, Brown's Secretary of War, was one of the killed. William H. Leeman, one of Brown's captains being pursued by scores, plunged into the river, a Virginian wading after him. Leeman turned round, threw up his empty hands, and cried, "Don't shoot!" The Virginian fired his pistol directly in the youth's face —he was but twenty-two—and shattered his head into fragments.

By this time, all the houses around the Armory building were held by the Virginians. Capt. Turner, who had fired the first shot in the morning, was killed by the sentinel at the Arsenal gate, as he was raising a rifle to fire. Here Dangerfield Newby, a

Virginia slave, and Jim, one of Col. Washington's negroes, with a free negro who had lived on Washington's estate, were shot dead; and Oliver Brown, another of the old man's sons, being hit by a ball, came inside of the gate, as his brother Watson had done, lay quietly down without a word, and in a few moments was dead. Mr. Beckham, mayor of the town, who came within range of the insurgents' rifles as they were exchanging volleys with the Virginians, was likewise killed.

Thompson, their prisoner, was attacked by scores of them in the parlor where he was confined, but saved for the moment by a young lady throwing herself between him and their presented rifles, because, as she afterward explained, she "did not want the carpet spoiled." He was dragged out to the bridge, there shot in cold blood, and his body riddled with balls at the base of the pier, whither he had fallen forty feet from the bridge.

By this time more militia had arrived from every quarter, and a party from Martinsburgh, led by a railroad conductor, attacked the Armory building in the rear, while a detachment of the same force assailed them in front. Brown, seeing that his enemies were in overwhelming force, repulsed his assailants, who lost two killed and six wounded.

Still, militia continued to pour in; the telegraph and railroad having been completely repaired, so that the Government at Washington, Gov. Wise at Richmond, and the authorities at Baltimore, were in immediate communication with Harper's Ferry, and hurrying forward troops from all quarters to overwhelm the remaining handful of insurgents, whom terror and rumor had multiplied to twenty times their actual number. At five p. m., Capt. Simms arrived, with militia from Maryland, and completed the investment of the Armory buildings, whence eighteen prisoners had already been liberated upon the retreat of Brown to the engine-house. Col. Baylor was commander-in-chief. The firing ceased at night-fall. Brown offered to liberate his prisoners, upon condition that his men should be permitted to cross the bridge in safety, which was refused. Night found Brown's forces reduced to four unwouned beside himself, with perhaps half a dozen negroes from the vicinity. Eight of the insurgents were already dead; another lay dying beside the survivors; two were captives mortally wounded, and one other unhurt. Around the few survivors were fifteen hundred armed, infuriated foes. Half a dozen of the party who had been sent out at early morning by Brown to capture slaveholders, and liberate slaves, were absent, and unable, even if willing, to rejoin their chief. They fled during the night to Maryland and Pennsylvania; but two of them were ultimately captured. During the night, Col. Lee, with ninety United States marines and two pieces of artillery, arrived and took possession of the Armory very close to the engine-house.

Brown, of course, remained awake and alert through the night, discomfited and beyond earthly hope, but perfectly cool and calm.

"Col. Washington said that Brown was the coolest man he ever saw in defying death and danger. With one son dead by his side, and another shot through, he felt the pulse of his dying son with one hand, held his rifle with the other, and commanded his men with the utmost composure, encouraging them to be firm, and to sell their lives as dearly as possible."

Conversing with Col. Washington during that solemn night, he said he had not pressed his sons to join him in this expedition, but did not regret their loss—they had died in a good cause.

At seven in the morning, after a parley which resulted in nothing, the marines advanced to the assault, broke in the door of the engine-house by using a ladder as a battering-ram, and rushed into the building. One of the defenders was shot and two marines wounded; but the odds were too great; in an instant, all resistance was over. Brown was struck in the face with a sabre and knocked down, after which the blow was several times repeated, while a soldier ran a bayonet twice into the old man's body. All the insurgents would have been killed on the spot, had the Virginians been able to distinguish them with certainty from their prisoners.

Of course, all Virginia, including her Governor, rushed to Harper's Ferry upon learning that all was over, and the insurrection completely suppressed. The bleeding survivors were subjected to an alterna-

tion of queries, which they met bravely as
they had confronted the bullets of their
numerous and ever-increasing foes.  They
answered frankly, and none of them sought
to conceal the fact that they had struck for
Universal Freedom at all hazards.  The
bearing of Brown was especially praised by
his enemies (many of whom won notoriety
in the ranks of the Rebellion).

C. L. Vallandigham, of Ohio, visited
Brown and on his return home, he said:

"It is in vain to underrate either the man
or the conspiracy.  Capt. John Brown is as
brave and resolute a man as ever headed
an insurrection.  He has coolness, daring,
persistency, the stoic faith and patience, and
a firmness of will and purpose unconquer-
able.  He is the farthest possible removed
from the ordinary ruffian, fanatic, or mad-
man.  Certainly, it was one of the best-
planned and best-executed conspiracies that
ever failed."

Brown and his four men, Stevens, Coppoc, Copeland and Green, were placed in
the old jail at Charleston, eight miles from
Harper's Ferry, about 5 o'clock in the afternoon on the day of their capture.  Cook
and Hazlett were captured in Pennsylvania

soon after. It is not necessary to speak of the legal proceedings in the case, that the conviction and death of Brown and his associates were pre-determined, is quite probable; and, Virginia had but this alternative —to hang John Brown, or to abolish slavery. She did not choose to abolish slavery and she had no other choice but to hang Brown, and as to trying him and Stevens while still weak and not able to stand up, it must be considered that the whole state was terror-stricken by the first news of their attempt, and that fears of insurrection and of an armed rescue were widely prevalent.

Brown's conduct throughout commanded the admiration of his bitterest enemies.

## ADDRESS OF PRESIDENT LINCOLN AT GETTYSBURG.

"Four score and seven years ago our fathers brought forth on this continent a new nation, conceived in liberty and dedicated to the proposition that all men are created equal. Now we are engaged in a great civil war, testing whether that nation, or any nation so conceived and so dedicated, can long endure. We are met on a great battlefield of the war. We have come to dedicate a portion of that field as a final resting-place for those who here gave up their lives that the nation might live. It is altogether fitting and proper that we should do this. But, in a larger sense we cannot dedicate—we cannot consecrate — we cannot hallow this ground. The brave men, living and dead, who struggled here, have consecrated it far above our power to add to detract. The world will little note or long remember what we say here, but it never can forget what they did here. It is for us, the living, rather to be dedicated here to the unfinished work which they who fought here have thus far so nobly carried on. It is rather for us to be dedicated to the great task remaining before us, that from these honored dead we take increased devotion to that cause for which they gave the last full measure of devotion; that we here highly resolve that these dead shall not have died in vain; that this nation, under God shall have a new birth of freedom, and that the Government of the people, by the people and for the people, shall not perish from the earth."

John Brown's Fort Monument at Harper's Ferry, marking the spot where his Fort stood before it was taken to the Chicago World's Fair. The Government placed this Monument here; also the five following tablets marking the spot where the Government Arsenal stood at the time John Brown held it, they describe the capture of Harper's Ferry in full.

# CAPTURE OF HARPER'S FERRY.

## SEPTEMBER 15.1862

### NO.1.

ON SEPTEMBER 10, 1862, GENERAL R.F. LEE, COMMANDING THE ARMY OF NORTHERN VIRGINIA, THEN AT FREDERICK MD. SET THREE COLUMS IN MOTION TO CAPTURE HARPER'S FERRY. MAJ. GEN. L. MC. LAWS WITH HIS OWN DIVISION AND THAT OF MAJ. GEN. R.H. ANDERSON, MARCHED THROUGH MIDDLETOWN AND BROWNSVILLE PASS INTO PLEASANT VALLEY. ON THE 12TH THE BRIGADES OF KERSHAW AND BARKSDALE ASCENDED MARYLAND HEIGHTS BY SOLOMONS GAP, MOVED ALONG THE CHEST AND, AT NIGHTFALL WERE CHECKED BY THE UNION FORCES UNDER COMMAND OF COL. THFORD, ABOUT TWO MILES NORTH OF THIS. EIGHT CONFEDERATE BRIGADES HELD WEVERTON SANDY HOOK AND APPROACHES FROM THE EAST. ON THE 13TH KERSHAW AND BARKSDALE DROVE THE UNION TROOPS FROM THE HEIGHTS FORD, ABANDON- ING SEVEN GUNS, RETREATED ACROSS THE PONTOON BRIDGE, A FEW YARDS ABOVE THE RAILROAD BRIDGE TO HARPERS FERRY. THE UNION LOSS WAS 38 KILLED, 134 WOUNDED. CONFEDERATE LOSS. 35 KILLED. 178 WOUNDED.

BRIG. GEN. JOHN G. WALKER'S DIVISION CROSSED THE POTOMAC AT POINT OF ROCKS, 10 MILES BELOW THIS, DURING THE NIGHT OF SEPTEMBER 10. AND, ON THE 13TH OCCUPIED LOUDOUN HEIGHTS AND THE ROADS SOUTH OF THE RIVER LEADING EAST AND SOUTH.

# CAPTURE OF HARPER'S FERRY,

## SEPTEMBER 15, 1862.

## No. 2.

MAJ. GEN. THOMAS J. JACKSON, WITH HIS OWN DIVISION AND THOSE OF MAJ. GENS. A. P. HILL AND R. S. EWELL, LEFT FREDERICK ON THE MORNING OF SEPTEMBER 10 AND PASSING THROUGH MIDDLETOWN AND BOONSBORO, CROSSED THE POTOMAC AT WILLIAMSPORT, 21 MILES NORTH OF THIS, ON THE AFTERNOON OF THE 11TH. HILL'S DIVISION TOOK THE DIRECT ROAD TO MARTINSBURG AND BIVOUACKED NEAR IT. JACKSON'S AND EWELL'S DIVISIONS MARCHED TO NORTH MOUNTAIN DEPOT ON THE BALTIMORE AND OHIO RAIL-ROAD, SEVEN MILES NORTHWEST OF MARTINSBURG, AND BIVOUACKED DURING THE NIGHT. BRIG. GEN. JULIUS WHITE, COMMANDING THE UNION TROOPS AT MARTINSBURG, ABOUT 2,500 IN NUMBER, ABANDONED THE PLACE AND RETREATED TO HARPER'S FERRY. JACKSON OCCUPIED MARTINS-BURG ON THE MORNING OF THE 12TH, PASSED THROUGH IT AND ABOUT NOON OF THE 13TH, A. P. HILL'S DIVISION IN THE ADVANCE, REACHED HALLTOWN, 3¾ MILES WEST OF THIS, AND WENT INTO CAMP. JACKSONS AND EWELL'S DIVISION, FOLLOWING HILL'S, ENCAMPED NEAR IT.

# CAPTURE OF HARPER'S FERRY.

## SEPTEMBER 15, 1862.

## NO.3.

COL. DIXON S. MILES, SECOND U.S. INFANTRY, COMMANDED THE UNION FORCES AT HARPER'S FERRY. AFTER GENERAL WHITE JOINED FROM MARTINSBURG, SEPTEMBER 12, AND COLONEL FORD FROM MARYLAND HEIGHTS ON THE 13TH, MILES HAD ABOUT 14,200 MEN. ON THE MORNING OF THE 14TH THE GREATER PART OF THIS FORCE WAS IN POSITION ON BOLIVAR HEIGHTS, 1⅝ MILES WEST, ITS RIGHT RESTING ON THE POTOMAC, ITS LEFT NEAR THE SHENANDOAH; ARTILLERY DISTRIBUTED ON THE LINE. ARTILLERY AND A SMALL FORCE OF INFANTRY OCCUPIED CAMP HILL, NEARLY MIDWAY BETWEEN THIS AND BOLIVAR HEIGHTS. THE CAVALRY WAS UNDER PARTIAL COVER OF THE IRREGULARITIES OF THE GROUND.

ON THE MORNING OF THE 14TH WALKER PLACED FIVE LONG RANGE GUNS NEAR THE NORTHERN POINT OF LOUDON HEIGHTS, AND AT 1 P.M. OPENED ON THE UNION BATTERIES ON BOLIVAR HEIGHTS AND CAMP HILL, WHICH WAS REPLIED TO. AN HOUR LATER JACKSON'S ARTILLERY OPENED ON BOLIVAR HEIGHTS FROM SCHOOL HOUSE HILL AND STILL AN HOUR LATER, McLAWS OPENED FROM TWO PARROTT GUNS THAT HE HAD SUCCEEDED IN PLACING NEAR THE SOUTHERN EXTREMITY OF MARYLAND HEIGHTS. THE FIRE FROM THESE THREE DIRECTIONS WAS CONTINUED UNTIL DARK, SILENCING AND DISMOUNTING SOME OF THE UNION GUNS.

# CAPTURE OF HARPER'S FERRY.

## SEPTEMBER 15, 1862.

### NO. 4.

IN THE AFTERNOON OF THE 14TH JACKSON'S DIVISION ADVANCED ITS LEFT,
SEIZED COMMANDING GROUND NEAR THE POTOMAC AND ESTABLISHED ARTIL-
LERY UPON IT. HILL'S DIVISION MOVED FROM HALLTOWN OBLIQUELY TO
THE RIGHT UNTIL IT STRUCK THE SHENANDOAH, THEN PUSHED ALONG THE
RIVER; THE ADVANCE, AFTER SOME SHARP SKIRMISHING LATE IN THE NIGHT
GAINED HIGH GROUND UPON WHICH WERE PLACED FIVE BATTERIES. COMMAND-
ING THE LEFT REAR OF THE UNION LINE. EWELL'S DIVISION ADVANCED
THROUGH HALLTOWN TO SCHOOL HOUSE HILL AND DEPLOYED ABOUT ONE
MILE IN FRONT OF BOLIVAR HEIGHTS, BIVOUACKING ON EITHER SIDE OF THE
CHARLESTOWN ROAD. DURING THE NIGHT THE CONFEDERATES ADVANCED
ON THE RIGHT AND LEFT GAINING SOME GROUND, AND 10 GUNS OF EWELL'S
DIVISION CROSSED THE SHENANDOAH AT KEY'S FORD AND WERE PLACED ON
THE PLATEAU AT THE FOOT OF LOUDON HEIGHTS TO ENFILADE THE
ENTIRE POSITION ON BOLIVAR HEIGHTS.

ABOUT 9 P.M. THE ENTIRE UNION CAVALRY FORCE, ABOUT 1500 MEN,
CROSSED THE PONTOON BRIDGE, PASSED UP THE CANAL BANK ABOUT A MILE,
FOLLOWED THE MOUNTAIN ROAD NEAR THE RIVER, CROSSED THE ANTIETAM
NEAR ITS MOUTH, PASSED THROUGH SHARPSBURG ABOUT MIDNIGHT AND
ESCAPED INTO PENNSYLVANIA.

# CAPTURE OF HARPER'S FERRY.

## SEPTEMBER 15, 1862.

## No.5

AT DAYLIGHT, SEPTEMBER 15, THREE BATTERIES OF JACKSONS DIVISION DELIVERED A SEVERE FIRE AGAINST THE RIGHT OF THE BOLIVAR HEIGHTS DEFENCE EWELL'S BATTERIES OPENED FROM SCHOOL HOUSE HILL IN FRONT. HILL'S FIVE BATTERIES ON GROUND COMMANDING THE LEFT OF THE LINE AND THE 10 GUNS ACROSS THE SHENANDOAH POURED AN ACCURATE ENFILADE FIRE UPON THE LEFT AND REAR OF MILES DEFENSES.  THE ARTILLERY ON LOUDOUN HEIGHTS AND MARYLAND HEIGHTS JOINED IN THE ATTACK. THIS CONCENTRATED FIRE OF 56 GUNS WAS RESPONDED TO BY THE UNION GUNS, BUT, IN AN HOUR BEGINNING TO RUN SHORT OF AMMUNITION MILES RAISED THE WHITE FLAG IN TOKEN OF SURRENDER. SOON AFTER HE WAS MORTALLY WOUNDED AND THE COMMAND DEVOLVED ON GENERAL WHITE WHO COMPLETED THE TERMS OF CAPITULATION BY THE SURRENDER OF ABOUT 12,500 OFFICERS AND MEN AND ALL PUBLIC PROPERTY. MILLS DIVISION WAS LEFT TO PAROLE THE PRISONERS WHILE JACKSON WITH FIVE DIVISIONS MARCHED TO THE FIELD OF ANTIETAM. EXCLUSIVE OF THE LOSS ON MARYLAND HEIGHTS. THE UNION LOSS WAS 9 KILLED 39 WOUNDED. CONFEDERATE LOSS 6 KILLED, 69 WOUNDED.

The above picture explains how the government has the John Brown fort, the monument and the tablets arranged ot Harper's Ferry.

# SONGS

I will now repeat the first two verses and chorus of the John Brown Song, which was composed at that time by a gentleman from Frederick, Maryland, and reads as follows:

## JOHN BROWN SONG.

In old Virginia there is a place they call it Charlestown,
    Where they hung an Abolitionist, his name was John Brown;
He came to Harper's Ferry, in the middle of the night,
    And thought to scare the citizens by showing them some fight.

CHORUS:

Now old John Brown, can't you never see,
    It will never do for you to try to set the negroes free?
For if you do, the people will come from all around—
    They will take you down and hang you up in old Charlestown.

Just then a train of cars came by,
   Making such a clatter, when out jumps
      the conductor,
And asks what is the matter, says Mr.
      Brown, to Conductor Phelps,
   "Don't you move or stir, for if you do, I
      will shoot you down,
As sure as you are here."

## THE OLD SONG.

John Brown's body lies a-mouldering in the
      grave;
John Brown's body lies a-mouldering in the
      grave;
John Brown's body lies a-mouldering in the
      grave;
   But his soul is marching on.

   CHORUS:
      Glory, glory, hallelujah!
      Glory, glory, hallelujah!
      Glory, glory, hallelujah!
      His soul is marching on.

He's gone to be a soldier in the army of
     the Lord;
He's gone to be a soldier in the army of
     the Lord;
He's gone to be a soldier in the army of
     the Lord;
     But his soul is marching on.

John Brown's knapsack is strapped upon
     his back;
John Brown's knapsack is strapped upon
     his back;
John Brown's knapsack is strapped upon
     his back;
     But his soul is marching on.

His pet lambs will meet him on the way;
His pet lambs will meet him on the way;
His pet lambs will meet him on the way;
     As they go marching on.

They will hang Jeff Davis on a sour apple
     tree;
They will hang Jeff Davis on a sour apple
     tree;
They will hang Jeff Davis on a sour apple
     tree;
     As they march along.

Now three rousing cheers for the Union!
Now three rousing cheers for the Union!
Now three rousing cheers for the Union!
　As they are marching on.

CHORUS:
　　　Glory, glory, hallelujah!
　　　Glory, glory, hallelujah!
　　　Glory, glory, hallelujah!
　　　Hip, hip, hip, hip-hurrah!